SNAKES

King Snakes

by Linda George

Consultants:
The staff of Black Hills Reptile Gardens
Rapid City, South Dakota

CAPSTONE
HIGH-INTEREST
BOOKS

an imprint of Capstone Press
Mankato, Minnesota

Capstone High-Interest Books are published by Capstone Press
151 Good Counsel Drive, P.O. Box 669, Mankato, Minnesota 56002
http://www.capstone-press.com

Library of Congress Cataloging-in-Publication Data
George, Linda.
King snakes/by Linda George.
p. cm.—(Snakes)
Includes bibliographical references (p. 45) and index.
ISBN 0-7368-0908-2
1. Lampropeltis—Juvenile literature. [1. King snakes. 2. Snakes.] I. Title.
II. Animals and the environment. Snakes.
QL666.O636 G46 2002
597.96'2—dc21   2001000046

Summary: Describes the physical attributes, habitat, and hunting and mating methods
of king snakes.

Editorial Credits
Blake Hoena, editor; Lois Wallentine, product planning editor; Timothy Halldin, cover
designer and illustrator; Katy Kudela, photo researcher

Photo Credits
Alan Blake Sheldon, 6, 18–19, 26, 38
Alan Blake Sheldon/Root Resources, 13
Brian Parker/TOM STACK & ASSOCIATES, 34
G and C Merker/Visuals Unlimited, 14, 17, 44
Jim Merli/Visuals Unlimited, 9
Joe McDonald/TOM STACK & ASSOCIATES, cover, 24
Joe McDonald/Visuals Unlimited, 33, 41
Michael Cardwell/Extreme Wildlife Photography, 37
Rick & Nora Bowers/Visuals Unlimited, 30
Unicorn Stock Photos/Dede Gilman, 10; Tommy Dodson, 20, 23;
    Russell R. Grunke, 29

1 2 3 4 5 6 07 06 05 04 03 02

Table of Contents

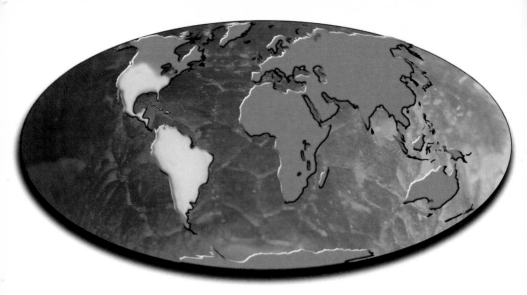

Yellow areas represent the king snake's range.

Fast Facts about King Snakes

Scientific Name:	King snakes are members of the *Lampropeltis* genus. This scientific group also includes milk snakes and mole snakes.
Size:	Most king snakes are between 1.5 and 6 feet (.5 and 1.8 meters) long.
Range:	King snakes live throughout much of the United States, Mexico, and South America.

Description:	King snakes are among the most colorful snakes. They can be a variety of colors and patterns. Some king snakes are similar in color to venomous coral snakes.
Habitat:	King snakes live near lakes, canals, streams, and farmlands. They also may live in wooded areas or pine barrens.
Food:	King snakes eat snakes, lizards, rodents, frogs, and birds.
Habits:	King snakes are constrictors. They kill prey by squeezing it. King snakes often eat other snakes. They sometimes eat venomous snakes. King snakes are not affected by the venom produced by these snakes.
Reproduction:	King snakes are oviparous. Female king snakes lay eggs that develop and hatch outside their bodies. Female king snakes usually lay between three and 24 eggs.

CHAPTER 1

King Snakes

King snakes are well known for one of their eating habits. They are ophiophagous. They eat other snakes. King snakes may even eat venomous snakes. They are not affected by the venom produced by these snakes.

Colubridae Family

Snakes are reptiles. Alligators, crocodiles, lizards, and turtles also are reptiles.

More than 2,300 snake species exist in the world. A species is a specific type of animal or plant.

Scientists divide snake species with similar features into families. King snakes belong to

King snakes are members of the Colubridae family.

the Colubridae family. This family is the largest snake family. It includes more than 1,000 snake species. Most snakes in this family are non-venomous. They vary greatly in color, size, and shape. Rat snakes, whip snakes, and racers also are members of the Colubridae family.

Lampropeltis Genus

Scientists further divide snake families into genera. King snakes are members of the *Lampropeltis* genus. This group also includes milk snakes and mole snakes.

Snakes within the *Lampropeltis* genus have smooth scales. They are non-venomous. These snakes are constrictors. They squeeze their prey to death. They also are known for eating other snakes.

King snakes have smooth scales.

CHAPTER 2

King Snake Species

The *Lampropeltis* genus includes more than 30 king snake species and subspecies. Scientists sometimes divide closely related snakes into subspecies. These snakes often differ in coloring. Most subspecies are located in one specific area or region.

Common King Snake

The common king snake's scientific name is *Lampropeltis gentulus*. Common king snakes usually are black or dark brown with narrow yellow or white bands. These bands split on the snake's sides and connect in a chainlike pattern on its underbelly. Common king snakes

Common king snakes are the largest king snake species.

sometimes are called "chain snakes" because of this color pattern.

The common king snake is the largest king snake species. It can grow to be 6 to 7 feet (1.8 to 2.1 meters) long.

California King Snake

The California king snake's scientific name is *Lampropeltis gentulus californiae*. This snake is a subspecies of the common king snake.

California king snakes can have a variety of color patterns. They can be black with cream-colored bands or brown with yellow bands. Some California king snakes have stripes that run lengthwise down their body. These snakes may be black with white stripes or brown with yellow stripes.

Most California king snakes grow to be about 3 feet (.9 meter) long. Some of these snakes grow to be more than 4 feet (1.2 meters).

Florida King Snake

The Florida king snake's scientific name is *Lampropeltis gentulus floridana*. This snake is a subspecies of the common king snake. The

California king snakes can be brown with yellow stripes.

Florida king snake is closely related to the California king snake.

Florida king snakes have yellow and brown scales. This coloring gives Florida king snakes a polka dot pattern. Florida king snakes' scales sometimes have red-brown or bright red centers. They have a cream to pale yellow underbelly with pink-brown or tan spots.

The scales on Florida king snakes form a polka dot pattern.

Florida king snakes usually are about the same length as California king snakes. They seldom measure more than 4 feet (1.2 meters) in length.

Scarlet King Snake
The scarlet king snake's scientific name is *Lampropeltis triangulun elapsoides*. This

snake is one of the smallest king snake species. Scarlet king snakes grow to be about 18 inches (46 centimeters) long.

Scarlet king snakes have brightly colored bands of red, yellow, and black around their body. These color markings are similar to venomous coral snakes. But the black bands are between the red and yellow bands on scarlet king snakes and other non-venomous snakes. On coral snakes, the red and yellow bands are side by side. Several sayings help people tell the difference between coral snakes and non-venomous snakes. One saying is "red and yellow kill a fellow."

Some scientists believe that there is a protective reason non-venomous snakes developed these color patterns. Predators may avoid coral snakes and other snakes that they recognize as dangerous. Predators also may avoid scarlet king snakes and other snakes that look similar to venomous snakes. This type of coloring is called mimicry.

Milk snakes display an important example of mimicry. These snakes often are gray with brown blotches. But milk snakes look different in areas where coral snakes live. There, milk snakes have red, yellow, and black bands.

Gray-Banded King Snake

The gray-banded king snake's scientific name is *Lampropeltis alterna*. Gray-banded king snakes are gray with black bands. Some gray-banded king snakes have a bright orange patch on the back of their head.

Some gray-banded king snakes have other color patterns. They may have bands of gray, white, black, and orange. Others may have black, white, and gray bands.

Gray-banded king snakes average 30 inches (76 centimeters) in length. They have a thin body and a wide head.

Gray-banded king snakes may have gray, white, black, and orange bands.

Bands

Head

Scarlet King Snake

Tail

CHAPTER 3

Habitat

King snakes live only in the Western Hemisphere. They are found throughout most of North and South America. These continents sometimes are referred to as the "New World." Because of this name, scientists often call king snakes "New World Colubrids."

Common King Snakes

Common king snakes live throughout most of the United States. They also can be found in parts of northern Mexico.

Common king snakes often live in wooded areas.

Common king snakes live in a variety of habitats. They live in forest, woodland, marsh, grassland, and desert areas. They often can be found hiding in thick vegetation, near water, or hiding under rocks and logs.

Western King Snakes

California king snakes live in rocky areas, brush-covered hillsides, and semi-desert areas. They can be found from California north to Oregon. They live as far east as Arizona and Utah.

Gray-banded king snakes can be found in the Chihuahuan Desert of northern Mexico. This desert extends into Arizona, New Mexico, and Texas. Gray-banded king snakes live in arid to semi-humid habitats. These areas include deserts and mountains.

Eastern King Snakes

Scarlet king snakes live from North Carolina and Kentucky south to Florida and Louisiana.

California king snakes often live in rocky areas.

They are burrowing snakes. They can be found under the loose bark of fallen and rotting trees. Scarlet king snakes are reclusive. They often hide. People seldom see scarlet king snakes in the open except at night when the snakes hunt.

Florida king snakes live mostly in Florida. But they also can be found in southern Georgia. Their habitats include areas near canals, lakes, and streams. They often are found in and around sugar cane fields and farmlands.

Florida king snakes live mostly in Florida.

CHAPTER 4

Hunting

King snakes are known for being ophiophagous. They eat other snakes. But king snakes also eat reptiles such as lizards and turtles. They may eat eggs, frogs, fish, insects, or earthworms. Many king snakes eat rodents such as mice and rats.

Hunting Habits

California king snakes are crepuscular. They hunt just after the sun sets. Their prey includes other snakes, mice, birds, and lizards.

Scarlet and Florida king snakes eat a variety of prey. Scarlet king snakes eat small snakes and lizards. They also may eat young mice, small

King snakes may eat rodents.

fish, insects, and earthworms. Florida king snakes eat lizards, small snakes, and rodents.

Gray-banded king snakes are nocturnal. They hunt at night for lizards, snakes, frogs, and small rodents.

Senses for Hunting

King snakes cannot see as well as people do. But they can detect movement, light, colors, and shapes. This ability helps king snakes find prey.

King snakes cannot hear as well as people do. Instead, they feel vibrations in the ground and air. These sensations help king snakes know when prey is near.

The Jacobson's organ is located on the roof of a king snake's mouth. Snakes use this organ to smell. A king snake flicks out its tongue to collect scent particles in the air or on the ground. The tongue carries the scents to the Jacobson's organ. A king snake can smell prey with its Jacobson's organ. A male king snake can smell females that are ready to mate.

King snakes use their tongues to help them smell.

Constriction

King snakes have teeth that curve toward the back of their mouth. This shape helps them hold onto prey once they catch it.

King snakes are constrictors. After catching prey, they wrap their muscular body around it. They then squeeze their prey. King snakes

squeeze tighter each time their prey breathes out. Squeezing prevents prey from breathing in. The prey then suffocates.

King snakes only need a few minutes to kill small prey. Some prey such as other snakes may take king snakes several hours to kill.

Preying on Snakes

King snakes are not affected by the venom of many venomous snakes. This immunity allows them to hunt rattlesnakes and cottonmouths. King snakes also eat non-venomous snakes such as rat snakes and other king snakes.

Venomous snakes use different methods to defend themselves against king snakes. Venomous snakes usually bite to defend themselves. But they may bite themselves while struggling with a king snake. Most snakes are not immune to their own venom and can die from their own bite.

King snakes are constrictors.

Instead of biting, venomous snakes raise their midsection when confronting a king snake. Venomous snakes bat at the king snake with this loop of their body. Scientists believe this action is meant to confuse the attacking king snake. But it seldom works. Venomous snakes then may bite as a last choice.

Swallowing Prey

King snakes do not chew their food. They swallow prey whole.

A king snake can swallow prey larger than its mouth. A king snake's upper and lower jaws are connected by ligaments. These stretchy bands of tissue allow a king snake to separate its jaws. Strong muscles in its throat then pull prey into its stomach.

A king snake may eat a snake as large as itself. The prey folds up inside the king snake's stomach as it is swallowed.

Strong acids in a king snake's stomach digest its prey. These chemicals break down

King snakes swallow their prey head first.

food to be used by the body. After a large meal, a king snake may not eat again for several months.

CHAPTER 5

Mating

Snakes are cold blooded. Their body temperature is similar to the temperature of their surroundings.

King snakes that live in cold climates must hibernate to survive. They burrow underground and remain inactive during winter. This inactivity allows king snakes to survive cold weather and lack of food.

King snakes wake from hibernation in spring. They then seek a mate. Female king snakes give off a scent that attracts male king snakes. This scent tells males that the females are ready to mate.

Female king snakes lay eggs.

Combat Dance

The female's scent may attract more than one male. Male king snakes then take part in a combat dance. This action decides which male mates with the female.

The dance starts when one male king snake tries to crawl past or over another male. The snakes then wrap their bodies around each other. They raise their heads and the front halves of their bodies high into the air. They do not bite each other during this dance. Instead, they try to climb on top of each other.

Eventually, one snake succeeds and holds the other one down for a moment. The losing king snake then leaves. The winning male mates with the female.

Laying Eggs

King snakes are oviparous. Female king snakes lay eggs that develop and hatch outside their body. Females lay between three and 24 eggs. The eggs hatch in late summer. Young king snakes are about 8 to 12 inches (20 to 30 centimeters) long.

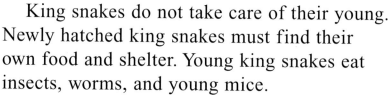

King snakes' eggs hatch in late summer.

King snakes do not take care of their young. Newly hatched king snakes must find their own food and shelter. Young king snakes eat insects, worms, and young mice.

Most young king snakes are darker in color than adult king snakes. This coloring makes them less visible to predators. As they grow older, their colors become brighter.

CHAPTER 6

King Snakes and People

Many myths exist about snakes. These stories are not true. One myth led to the name "milk snake."

Some dairy farmers noticed a decline in their cows' milk production. These farmers may have seen king snakes or milk snakes in their barns. The farmers then told stories that the snakes had milked their cows. In truth, the king snakes and milk snakes were probably in the barns searching for prey. Mice and rats often are found in and around farm buildings.

Some farmers thought that king snakes milked their cows.

King Snakes as Pets

Many people own king snakes as pets. They believe king snakes make better pets than most other snakes. King snakes become tame with handling. They also readily eat the food given to them.

Snakes often bite to defend themselves. But snake experts believe king snakes are mild-tempered. Tame king snakes rarely bite the people who handle them.

Benefits to People

King snakes are important to farmers. King snakes help keep rodent populations down by eating rats and mice. These animals may eat farmers' crops. Rodents also can carry many diseases to farm animals and food. By eating rodents, king snakes help prevent some diseases from spreading.

King snakes eat venomous snakes.

King snakes also eat venomous snakes, their eggs, and their young. They can help limit the population of venomous snakes in areas where people live.

Words to Know

acids (ASS-ids)—substances in an animal's stomach that break down food

crepuscular (kri-PUS-ku-lur)—active between sunset and nightfall

digest (dye-JEST)—to break down food so that it can be used by the body

family (FAM-uh-lee)—a group of animals with similar features

genus (JEE-nuhss)—a group of related animal or plant species

habitat (HAB-uh-tat)—the place and natural conditions in which plants and animals live

hibernate (HYE-bur-nate)—to be inactive during the winter; king snakes often hibernate by burrowing into the ground.

immune (i-MYOON)—not affected by; king snakes are immune to the venom of venomous snakes.

ligament (LIG-uh-muhnt)—a strong, stretchy band of tissue that connects bones

nocturnal (nok-TUR-nuhl)—active at night

ophiophagous (AH-fee-off-uh-gus)—a diet that includes snakes

oviparous (oh-VIP-uh-rus)—laying eggs that develop and hatch outside the female's body

prey (PRAY)—an animal hunted by another animal for food

species (SPEE-sheez)—a specific type of animal or plant

suffocate (SUHF-uh-kate)—to kill by cutting off the supply of air or oxygen

venom (VEN-uhm)—poison produced by some snakes; venom is passed into a victim's body when a venomous snake bites.

To Learn More

George, Linda. *Rat Snakes.* Snakes. Mankato, Minn.: Capstone High-Interest Books, 2002.

Ling, Mary, and Mary Atkinson. *The Snake Book.* New York: DK Publishing, 1997.

Mattison, Christopher. *Snake.* New York: DK Publishing, 1999.

Stone, Lynn M. *Snakes that Squeeze and Snatch.* Eye to Eye with Snakes. Vero Beach, Fla.: Rourke, 2000.

Useful Addresses

Black Hills Reptile Gardens
P.O. Box 620
Rapid City, SD 57709

Milwaukee Public Museum
Herpetology Department
800 West Wells Street
Milwaukee, WI 53233-1478

Smithsonian National Zoological Park
3001 Connecticut Avenue NW
Washington, DC 20008

Toronto Zoo
361A Old Firch Avenue
Scarborough, ON M1B 5K7
Canada

Internet Sites

Black Hills Reptile Gardens
http://www.reptile-gardens.com

Chaffee Zoological Gardens of Fresno–King Snakes
http://www.chaffeezoo.org/zoo/animals/
kingsnakes.html

Enchanted Learning.com–Snake Printouts
http://www.enchantedlearning.com/subjects/
reptiles/snakes/printouts.shtml

Toronto Zoo
http://www.torontozoo.com

Index